New Puppy, Now What?

Foundation Skills for Raising a Happy Puppy

Erica Marshall CPDT-KA

Copyright © 2021 Erica Marshall.

All rights reserved. No part of this publication may be reproduced, distributed, or transmitted in any form or by any means, including photocopying, recording, or other electronic or mechanical methods, without the prior written permission of the publisher, except in the case of brief quota-tions embodied in critical reviews and certain other noncommercial uses permitted by copyright law. For permission requests, write to the publisher, addressed "Attention: Permissions Coordina-tor," at the address below.

ISBN: 978-1-95386534-2 (Paperback)
ISBN: 978-1-95386535-9 (Ebook)

Library of Congress Control Number: 2021912478

Books Fluent
3014 Dauphine Street
New Orleans, LA
70117

Contents

5   **Introduction**

CHAPTER 1
7   **Puppy Development**
How do they grow?

CHAPTER 2
15   **Preparing For Your Puppy**
What Do You Need?

CHAPTER 3
25   **Building your Puppy's Professional Network**
All the People You and Your Puppy Need to Succeed!

CHAPTER 4
31   **Caring for The Whole Puppy**

CHAPTER 5
45   **Puppies and Kids**
How to Live in Peace Together

CHAPTER 6
51   **The Vital Basics**
Training for a Happy and Healthy Puppy

CHAPTER 7
83   **Foundation Training Games**
Skill Building Fun

99   **Resources**
105 **Author Thanks**

Introduction

Jojen and I training in the local park

Throughout my time working with families and their dogs, it has become clear to me that as a society and culture we sorely misunderstand the importance of the early life of a dog. Short of fretting about potty training and those sharp little puppy teeth, we don't give much thought to any other developmental needs of a puppy. This lack of focus on the early education of our puppies often results in problematic behavior issues in the adolescent years. I have built a business around this problematic behavior.

It is vitally important that as new owners we are thoughtful and intentional with puppies right from the start.

This book comes after many years developing a comprehensive puppy program to really get to the heart of what is important for puppies and their owners to learn right from the start. I have made it my mission to get the information out to everyone who needs it. Puppyhood is fleeting and there are so many things we want them to learn in such a short time. Most people try to pack it all in and can miss the really important fundamentals. I have spent years writing and re-writing training programs for puppies and inevitably it always comes down to the basic foundations. You can't teach a puppy to sit if he isn't even paying attention to you. You can't teach a puppy to come when called if he hasn't been taught how much fun you are. You can't teach your puppy to be happy to meet people if he's only met 4 people in his whole young life.

Raising a happy, well-adjusted adult dog is a marathon, not a sprint. Training doesn't stop after puppy class or at six months. It is a lifelong process. What makes the training journey so much easier is working on the foundations in a positive manner right from the start. Paring down and wading through all the behaviors you eventually want your dog to know. Of course sit and stay can be important but there is some real work that needs to happen beforehand that will make teaching sit and stay much easier and with greater reliability.

The most important part of raising a puppy is the relationship you build together. Bringing a puppy into your home is exciting, exhausting and entertaining. Your success in raising a happy, healthy and well-behaved dog is dependent on a relationship built on clear communication, trust and fun. The puppy phase goes quickly, there is plenty of time to learn sit and stay. Your focus should be on the joy of having a puppy and creating a strong foundation that all other important behaviors can be built on. This book will help you do that so you and your puppy can have many years together finding joy!

CHAPTER 1
Puppy Development
How do they grow?

Birth—2 weeks

Puppies are born blind, deaf and toothless. They are dependent on their mother and littermates to stay warm because they cannot regulate their own body temperature. Vocalizations are how they communicate to their littermates and mother. The mother stimulates urination and defecation by vigorously licking their bodies.

During this period puppies sleep about ninety percent of the time, waking only to nurse. Their birth weight should increase daily over these first two weeks.

They have clumsy movements and belly scoot around the whelping area. This helps develop their muscle strength and coordination. They are unable to support their own body weight at this time.

Their sense of smell and touch are their most developed senses at this point. They rely on these senses to navigate their environment and locate their mother and littermates. This is the time a breeder may introduce new scents to the air or whelping box to aid in mental and neurological stimulation. Body handling and stroking should be part of the socialization process as well.

2 weeks—4 weeks

Puppies go through great physical changes during this short time. Their ears begin to open at around 2 weeks, allowing for a greater response to environmental sounds. They may also develop louder vocalizations. This would be a great time to introduce new sounds to the whelping environment, such as rain, thunderstorms, soothing music, or talk radio. These "real life" sounds are a vital part of the socialization process.

Their eyes can open anywhere between 10-16 days old. Their vision is blurry at first, but will sharpen quickly, allowing them to make out shapes and objects. Vision helps them identify their siblings and mother in close proximity. This is when additions of new items or toys in the whelping area can help develop their vision and aid in the neurological and socialization development.

Puppies also begin to stand and support their weight on their legs at this stage. They get more mobile, although they are still quite clumsy in their movements. Play between littermates begins to happen around 3 weeks. They may begin to explore the whelping area, moving a bit further away from their mother than they did before. Their teeth begin to emerge, and they can be introduced to eating something other than mother's milk. They learn how to use their new teeth with their littermates, learning the vital art of bite inhibition. Between 3-4 weeks is also when they begin searching out areas away from their sleeping area to urinate and defecate -the start of potty training!

4 weeks-12 weeks

This is when socialization should be happening in earnest. Weeks 4-6 are punctuated by the mother beginning to wean the puppies and taking extended breaks from them. The puppies are exploring their environment more. This is the perfect time to introduce new and novel items to the environment for them to discover and explore. Things like scratchy mats for them to walk on or low balance items like blocks of wood to walk over or across. Sounds such as the vacuum cleaner, a baby crying, a tea kettle whistling etc. can also be introduced. Puppies should also be meeting new people to interact with at this time.

Their teeth are fully erupted by 6 weeks and they are continuing to learn how to control themselves through play with their littermates and mother.

Weaning by the mother is generally finished by 8 weeks and the puppies should be getting most of their nutrition from regular meals. Socialization should continue with meeting new people, body handling, new sounds and scents and sights. Being allowed to explore outside in a safe place is vital as well, and potty training can be expedited this way. Allowing puppies to explore, builds their neurological pathways and confidence in their surroundings.

8 weeks is the earliest a puppy should be removed from his mother and littermates. This means their new family needs to continue the socialization started by the breeder. If this is a rescue puppy with no known history, the new family should assume nothing and start from scratch. This time frame also coincides with a "fear period" where new things can elicit a fear response, such as whining, hiding or barking. The socialization technique used during this process can have a direct effect on the severity and length of this period.

At 8 weeks their growth plates are still open. This means that care needs to be taken with physical exertion and exercise. They are still clumsy in their body coordination and movements so vigorous walks, hikes or climbing -even stairs—can have a negative effect on their growth development and can possibly cause soft tissue injury or damage.

At 8 weeks a puppy may still need to urinate and defecate around the clock, but their bathroom habits can be predicted with careful observation and a regimented feeding schedule. A good rule of thumb to remember is that puppies generally need to go to the bathroom every hour, after eating, drinking, playing, and upon waking.

> 8 weeks is also the perfect time to start a puppy training class or have a trainer visit your home to get you started on a training and socialization plan. As long as your puppy has his first set of shots and you are careful about the places he visits and the dogs he meets, it is safe —and indeed vital —for him to get out and about in the world. The greatest threat to a dog's life is improper or under socialization, NOT contagious diseases.

12 weeks is the end of what is known as the "socialization window". It is important that you have prepared your puppy within these few short weeks as best you can. It doesn't stop here though! You can continue the lessons right up through full maturity at age two and even beyond! The better your beginning foundation though, the easier it will be going forward with your growing puppy.

4-6 months

This is the stage of development that has great physical growth and increased independence. A puppy's sleep and wake habits are more regular as are their potty habits. This is when continuing to attend training classes or private lessons with a trainer will pay off ten-fold as your puppy grows into adolescence and presents new challenges such as destructive chewing, jumping, counter surfing, running away etc. If you have been working with your puppy right along, these challenges will be easier to work with than if you just start at this stage. Patience is imperative in this stage of puppy development.

This is also when your puppy may experience a second fear period. It can be punctuated by your puppy suddenly being afraid of things that previously never bothered him or of new people or new sounds. Again, if you've put the early work in, this new development will be easier to get through.

Formal training in either a group or private setting should continue through at least your puppy's first year and preferably through full maturity and beyond. Training works their developing brain and keeps your puppy or adolescent dog engaged and gives him better ways to express his energy and needs. Formal training helps you to teach your puppy to ask to go outside by ringing a bell at the back door rather than peeing on the rug in front of it, or to go in his crate to chew on his bone rather than under the table to chew on the chair leg!

A litter of foster puppies learning to give attention to people

Finn shows us how puppies will entertain themselves if unsupervised!

Grates in the ground can be scary, Finn uses his nose to check it out. Allowing your dog to sniff things that may be strange to him allows him to make a determination if it's safe or not.

My daughter Caitie helps socialize a litter of foster puppies

Harper works her muscles playing on uneven terrain.

A sleeping Chinook puppy.

Chinook puppies sleeping in a pile.

Evie sweetly sleeping. Puppies need between 16-20 hours of sleep a day!

Introduction 13

CHAPTER 2
Preparing For Your Puppy

What Do You Need?

Lady, the cutest little English Bulldog ever!

If you haven't yet picked out the perfect puppy and are struggling to decide between the path of a rescue organization or a breeder, here are some strategies to help you make the right choice no matter which path you choose.

Choosing a Breeder

Choosing the right breeder can seem easy. Just pick your preferred breed, go online, do a search and pick the breeder with the cutest puppies. But if you want to make sure you are getting the healthiest puppy that is the best fit for your unique family, you need to do a little more than an online search.

1. Look up your preferred breed's breed club in or around your area. They will usually have a listing of breeders within driving distance of your home. You want one close enough so you can meet the breeder and their dogs. If you contact a breeder and they do not allow you to visit or you are only allowed to meet the puppies but not the mother, move on to another breeder. If you are not allowed to see the environment the puppies were raised in, move on. Meeting at least one of the parents is important to see the temperament the puppies come from. Seeing where they are raised is important in understanding the type of care and early socialization they will get while with the breeder.

2. Search for breeders that also work with their breed's rescue network. It will give you a good sense of their commitment to the breed and the animals, not just the income they bring in.

3. Be sure a breeder does breed appropriate health testing such as the Orthopedic Foundation for Animals, or OFA, testing for hips, knees, elbows, eyes, etc. If a breeder does no health testing short of a regular vet exam, look for another breeder.

4. Expect an in-depth questionnaire on your family life and expectations for your puppy. If you are looking for an all-around great family pet, a field line working dog may be the wrong choice and a good breeder can steer you in the right direction. If the breeder asks you no or only a few questions about your puppy's projected life or your home environment, find another breeder.

> See resources section for more information on OFA testing

5. Look for a breeder with a return guarantee for the life of the puppy. A good breeder takes responsibility for the puppies they bring into the world and are committed to them for life.

They should be happy to take a puppy back at any time, for any reason.

Choosing a Rescue Group

Choosing a good rescue group requires just as much due diligence as finding a breeder. If you want a specific breed, the breed clubs can point you in the right direction. If you are looking for a general rescue group, ask your friends and family who they got their dogs from and what their experience was. You may find a consensus and it'll be easy. If you are still not sure these tips can help you find a rescue that is right for you.

1. Research rescue groups in your area so you can meet the puppies before adoption. Many groups hold adoption events, these are great ways to meet the members of the organization and see the kinds of puppies and dogs they have in their rescue. If a rescue has a foster home network, you should be able to meet and speak with the foster person and meet the dog before making a decision to adopt. Adopting a puppy or dog before meeting them can be tricky. Try to avoid it if at all possible.

2. Look for a rescue that works with foster homes. Shelters can be a great place to find a puppy, but it's not guaranteed they will really know much about your chosen puppy. A foster home gives the puppy a chance to show his personality and any quirks he may have. Fosters can be very helpful in placing puppies into homes that are the right fit. Most fosters can also begin the potty training and crate training process for you, so you have a bit of a head start.

3. Look for a rescue that asks in depth questions about your daily home life and any expectations you may have for your puppy. A good rescue is excellent at matching prospective adopters with a puppy that will best fit into your lifestyle.

4. Choose a rescue that provides on-going support to their adopters as needed, including taking back one of their puppies for any reason at any time. A good rescue takes the

responsibility of placing puppies and dogs into homes very seriously and they are committed to them for their life.

5. Search for rescues that have a relationship with a trainer or has a training philosophy that is humane and based in current behavioral science and learning theory. If a rescue subscribes to the dominance hierarchy theory or alpha theory, find another rescue. These theories are no longer relevant and can actually cause more harm than good.

> Dominance theory has been refuted not only by the vast majority of the training and behavior community; it has also been refuted by the scientist that first introduced it to the world based on wolf behavior in captivity. For more information on why it is no longer part of the scientific study of dog behavior check the resources section at the back of the book.

Time to Shop

Now that you have welcomed a puppy into your home, it's time to go shopping! Don't break the bank buying every kind of toy, bed or treat you see. You don't want to overwhelm your puppy and it may take some time for you and your puppy to figure out what he likes best. If you have supplies from a previous pet, make sure they are in good condition and thoroughly cleaned before giving them to your puppy. Here's a shopping list to help you get started.

1. Stainless steel or ceramic food and water bowls.
2. Feeding mat to keep messes to a minimum.
3. Appropriate size Martingale or flat buckle collar.
4. A six-foot nylon or leather leash.
5. Appropriately sized soft body harness.

6. Crate large enough to accommodate your puppy's adult size. There should be a divider included to allow a purchase your puppy can grow into.

7. Crate pad or bedding, unless you know for sure they eat bedding.

8. Kong rubber toy that is one size larger than you think you need. This is the one product I recommend buying at least two of right off the bat.

9. Long rope or tug toy.

10. Stuffed toy.

11. Baby gate or exercise pen to make sure your puppy doesn't wander where he isn't allowed in the house.

12. ID tags. Identification on your puppy's collar is important. Even if he is microchipped, having visible identification can get him back to you much faster if he gets lost.

13. Puppy food. Look for a brand that fits your budget and still provides good quality.

> Choosing a food for your new puppy can be a daunting task. Talk to your veterinarian about the nutritional needs of a puppy. You can do brand comparisons at www.dogfoodadvisor.com

Puppy Proofing 101

To make sure your home is safe for your puppy it's important to look around, especially down low, and take care of any potentially dangerous situations. Here's a list to help you with this process:

1. Hide or secure any loose electrical cords as best as you can.

2. Gate off stairs —up or down —in the house.

3. Protect kids' bedrooms or playrooms with gates or exercise pens.

4. Tack up loose cords for blinds or curtains.

5. Keep your puppy in a smaller, easily cleanable area of the home while potty training.

6. Get low and look for any loose debris or items your puppy could chew or ingest.

7. Keep your puppy's food secure and out of reach.

8. Keep your puppy from having direct access to any door that leads outside unless it leads to a fenced or secured area.

> **Additional tips for products**
>
> Do not use plastic bowls. They can harbor bacteria even after washing.
>
> No choke chains or prong collars on puppy necks.
>
> No retractable leashes for puppies, there is too much risk of injury. A puppy hitting the end of a retractable leash can severely injure their neck and spine. If you must use one, ONLY use it for quick outside potty breaks, not for walks or playtime and it should be attached to a body harness not a collar.
>
> For information on harnesses check out the resources section.

9. Make sure all critter bait traps —both inside and out —have been moved away from your puppy's main area.

10. Chemicals kept in low level cabinets should be secured with a cabinet lock. Some ambitious puppies can figure out how to open cabinets.

11. Make sure your yard is free from any dangerous debris your puppy can chew, ingest or accidentally injure himself on.

12. Remove any valuable pieces of furniture or décor out of your puppy's immediate area -or at least block access with an exercise pen. You don't want him chewing on that antique chair!

13. Remove as many rugs as possible to make clean up as easy as can be expected.

Wally shows off what he was bred to do...run! It's important to allow your puppy to express his natural tendencies in a way that is safe.

Gabby shows just how important puppy proofing is!

Evie enjoys a very natural instinct to dig. Puppies dig to help alleviate boredom and because it is just plain fun. If you would like to discourage digging in certain places, you can create a digging spot just for your puppy.

A great assortment of Kong brain toys

Gabby enjoyed playing in the mud in her foster home

Ica explores climbing rocks

Finn sits near all his new fun puppy stuff!

CHAPTER 3
Building your Puppy's Professional Network

All the People You and Your Puppy Need to Succeed!

Find your Veterinarian

One of the first relationships you want to develop with a new puppy is with a veterinarian. If you already have a family veterinarian this will be easy, and you can just add your new puppy to your family file. If this is new territory for you, rest easy. Finding a veterinarian can seem daunting, but there are plenty of resources to help you. In addition to asking family and friends, you can do a Google search of your area. Make sure to look at their credentials, associations, hours, number of doctors, proximity to your home and accessibility after hours. Don't hesitate to make a meet and greet appointment so you can see if they are a right fit for

> You can look at The American Veterinary Medical Association at www.avma.org , The American Animal Hospital Association at www.aaha.org or Fear Free Pets at www.fearfreepets.com for what to look for in a potential vet or where to find one in your area.

you and your puppy. It is important to establish this relationship before your puppy comes home or very shortly thereafter to avoid scrambling to find one in an emergency.

Find your Trainer

Equally important is finding a trainer to help you and your puppy on your training journey. Formal training can happen as soon as your puppy comes home. Don't hesitate to get a trainer on board to make sure you are well prepared to start off on the right foot. As with your veterinarian, trying to find a suitable trainer is about finding the right fit for you and your family. The dog training industry is not currently regulated, so it is up to you to do some homework to find a trainer that can help you and your puppy in a way you are happy with. The best way to be sure that your puppy is getting help from a knowledgeable and experienced trainer is to look for these certifications: Certified Professional Dog Trainer Knowledge Assessed (CPDT-KA), Certified Professional Dog Trainer Knowledge and Skills Assessed (CPDT-KSA), Karen Pryor Academy Certified Training Partner (KPA-CTP), Associate Certified Dog Behavior Consultant (ACDBC), or Certified Dog Behavior Consultant (CDBC). These are the gold standards in the industry and also require trainers with these credentials to acquire continuing education credits to maintain certification.

> There are plenty of resources to help find a suitable trainer. The Association of Professional Dog Trainers at www.apdt.com, The Certification Council of Professional Dog Trainers at www.ccpdt.com and The International Association of Animal Behavior Consultants at www.iaabc.org all have trainer searches.

Find your Groomer

Not all puppies will need serious grooming, but it is still an excellent idea to find one that can help your puppy acclimate to the process should you ever need it, even if it's just for nail trims or

—heaven forbid —skunk smell removal! Ask your friends and family what groomer they love. People are very loyal to a great groomer. It is best if the groomer works on one pet at a time to minimize crate time and stress. Ask if you can make a short "get to know you" appointment so you can bring your puppy in, see the grooming set up and get a chance to chat with the groomer. This can be a big socialization opportunity for puppies between 8-12 weeks.

> Daycares can have specialized certifications as well. Certifications from organizations like the Professional Animal Care Certification Council at www.paccert.org are a huge plus.

Find Your Pet Care Team

Daycare

Not all dog daycares are created equal and not all are appropriate for puppies. You need to do your research, visit the facility at different times of the day, speak with the staff, read reviews, get opinions from family and friends and then decide if this option is right for you and your puppy. Make sure the place you choose has insurance and requires continuing education in the field of dog behavior for their staff.

> Dog walkers should carry some type of insurance and there are certification programs for dog walking. Check for credentials and certifications or continuing education.

Dog walker

There are lots of online organizations that provide these services. Beware of them. Allowing someone you've never met into your home to care for your puppy can be a dangerous situation. That being said, having a dog walker is a great option if you don't have a suitable daycare nearby or you choose not to use daycare. Again, ask family and friends or even your veterinarian, if they have recommendations. Have the dog walker come to the house to meet you and your puppy. Allow them to take your puppy outside to interact with each other. See how they handle all the puppy antics, even simple things like putting on a harness and leash.

Boarding or Pet sitting

Often, a dog walker and pet sitter are one in the same, and if you can find that, fantastic! If not, you'll want to decide if you want someone staying in your home, someone that takes your puppy into their home, or a formal boarding facility. If you choose to allow someone in your home, make sure they are properly insured, provide all contact information and have excellent references. If you leave your puppy in someone's home or a boarding facility make sure you can see where your puppy will be staying while in the facility or home setting. Will your puppy have regular outside access? Can the caregivers accommodate special feeding instructions, like feeding three times a day for young puppies? Are the caregivers able to give any medications that may be needed? What vaccines do they require? What are their pick-up and drop off hours? How much time will your puppy be alone? Do they have good references or reviews? Is the staff appropriately trained in medical emergencies? Do the dogs in their care seem clean, happy and healthy? If there are other staff or family members that will be interacting with your puppy, make sure you get to meet them as well.

The first day Percy and I met. We just spent time getting to know each other, building our bond.

Althea shows us that wonderful attention that is so important to get from your puppy.

CHAPTER 4
Caring for The Whole Puppy

Mental Stimulation-Keeping Your Puppy Entertained

You know the benefits of physical exercise for puppies, but did you know the benefits of mental exercise are just as important? Giving your puppy an opportunity to think, solve puzzles and learn has a huge effect on his quality of life and your sanity!

Any puppy, no matter the breed or breed mix, can learn to use their brain to solve puzzles, games and problems and it is in your best interest to channel that ability into something appropriate. Figuring out how to open their crate to let themselves out so they can tear up your couch, is indeed mental exercise, just not the kind we humans appreciate!

Brain toys help facilitate puppies to think and solve "problems" as well as give them appropriate outlets for chewing and to keep them safely occupied when you can't closely supervise them. There are many types of brain toys on the market now, below is a list of some of my favorites and their uses.

> See the Resources page for website listings for these great products!

Kong Products

Food Dispensing Toys

Classic Kong: The first and foremost brain toy to save the sanity of puppy owners everywhere! I like to keep multiple in the house and have them on a rotation when I have a puppy in my home. My favorite thing to do is whip up a concoction of my puppy's kibble, some plain yogurt or canned pumpkin. I stuff the Kong with a day's rations and then put it in the freezer. A frozen Kong for breakfast in my puppy's crate means I can get myself and my children ready for the day without worrying about what mischief my puppy is getting into. I do the same thing for dinnertime, so that I can make my dinner as well!

Kong Wobbler: This hard, plastic toy is another great way to feed your puppy his meal or just give him something to occupy himself.

Kong Gyro: This toy rolls and bounces, challenging puppies to figure out how best to make the food come out.

Classic Goodie Bone: This bone can be filled with food on either end for your puppy's enjoyment.

Kong Hopz Ball: This toy bounces and rocks making treat delivery unpredictable and keeps puppies engaged.

Interactive Toys: to play with together

Safe Stix: A much better alternative for a game of fetch than a real stick that can shed sharp pieces that can pierce mouths.

Bounzer: A fun bouncy odd shaped toy that can be tossed around and carried.

Kong Tug: A dual sided toy, great for playing tug between you and your puppy or between your puppy and their other canine friends.

Kong Wubba: A great toy for playing fetch or tug with.

Pet Safe Products

Food Dispensing Toys

Kibble Nibble: Another of my favorites for mealtime. This works well for the rambunctious puppies, as it's a great game to bang around this egg-shaped ball trying to get the kibble to fall out. This is also a great toy for those puppies that like to wolf down their food.

Twist-n-Treat: This hard rubber toy comes in two halves that can screw together. You can smear peanut butter or cream cheese and some kibble on each half and then screw it together. You can make the opening as wide or as narrow as you want. The tighter you screw the top down the more challenging it becomes for your puppy to get at the food. Experiment and see how much patience and perseverance your puppy has to determine his level of difficulty with this toy.

Barnacle: This multi-faceted toy can be stuffed with bits of kibble or treats in the three different size openings and the grooves on the outside can be smeared with peanut butter, canned dog food, coconut oil or squeeze cheese, to create a really enticing mental workout.

Tug-a-Jug: This is a kibble dispensing toy except it is a bit more challenging for the pups that need a bigger challenge. This hard, plastic jug has an opening at the top with a rope toy sticking out. Your puppy needs to figure out how to move the jug and rope around, so the food falls out. It can be frustrating for those puppies new to brain toys so it might be best to work up to this toy slowly.

Magic Mushroom: This is another odd shaped food dispensing toy that presents a great mental challenge and can serve as a way to feed your puppy his entire meal.

Nina Ottosson Products

Dog Puzzles Level 1&2

These brain-busting toys are made to challenge your puppy with a game of "find the treat." Your puppy has to move pieces around using any means possible to find the treat hidden in the compartments.

Dog Pyramid

Dog treat Maze

Dog Brick

Dog Miracle Puzzle

Dog Smart

Dog Finder

Dog Twister

Dog Casino

Fun Feeder Slo-Bowl

Brain Games on the Cheap

A muffin tin and some tennis balls: For a cheap and easy brain toy get an old muffin tin, place a small treat or piece of kibble in each cup then cover the cups with tennis balls. Your puppy has to figure out how to get the tennis balls out to get the treat underneath. You can even make it more challenging by only putting a treat in certain cups.

> The Fun Feeder Slo-Bowl is a great first puzzle for your puppy. It is designed to help slow down puppies that gulp their food, but it also creates just enough of a challenge to make your puppy work to get the food out. It comes in different sizes and shapes. See the Resources page for where to get it.

The cup game: Take three large plastic cups and place a treat or piece of kibble under each one. Tell your puppy to find it and watch as he figures out how to tip or shove over the cups to get the treat inside. Celebrate his cleverness, then increase the challenge by only hiding one treat and moving the cups around or not letting him watch what you are doing.

Chewing Toys

Antlers (deer, moose, elk)

Himalayan Chews (hard chew made from yak's milk)

Nylabone

Kong Firehose products

Tuffy dog toys

Safe Stix

Appropriate toys for Crate and Unsupervised Play

Nylabone

Classic Kong (filled with food)

Antler

Classic Kong Goodie Bone

Outdoor Toys

Tether-Tug

Kong Tug

Kong Safe Stix

Jolly Ball-Push-n-play

Jolly Egg

Jolly Ball Tug-n-Toss

Chuck It ball and throwing stick, water toys, frisbees

Holee Roller

Remember, challenging your puppy's brain is just as important as exercising his body. Using these toys and games can go a long way in strengthening your relationship, expending some energy on those bad weather days and giving you peace of mind when you can't closely supervise your puppy.

How to Exercise Your Puppy Properly

Exercise for a puppy needs to be approached carefully and with an understanding of their growing bodies. The saying "A tired puppy is a good puppy" is true, but you need to be careful about how you tire your puppy out.

Puppies growth plates are very delicate and too much repetitive or vigorous exercise can have a negative effect on his bone, ligament and muscle development. It can even cause injury. Generally, growth plates close by 6 months, but that can vary by breed.

Long distance walks, difficult hikes, sustained running or repetitive obstacle challenges can all have a detrimental effect on your puppy's growing body.

Of course, exercise is still necessary and important for your growing puppy but being mindful of letting your puppy lead the type and amount of exercise is your best bet. A leash walk up and down your driveway or on the sidewalk in front of your house is lengthy enough. Natural play in their yard or park is fantastic. Letting them play, run and climb up small rolling hills helps build stamina and muscle without overly stressing their joints and ligaments.

Repeated use of stairs at an early age can also cause stress on a puppy's growing body. It is best to carry your pup up and down stairs, at least until they are 5-6 months or too big to carry any longer. A couple stairs should be fine as long as they are taken slowly, even a small tumble can strain and overly exert growing ligaments and muscles or even break soft bones. Puppies are notoriously clumsy and uncoordinated. Decreasing the likelihood of injury by being careful is important. Large breed dogs can pose a dilemma as it is easy to forget how young a large breed puppy actually is because of their size. Slow and steady is the name of the game. Literally taking one step at a time with your puppy. Reward at each step, this will help slow the process down limiting the possibility of injury.

Puppies under 12 weeks should be taking leash walks no longer than your driveway. Their leashes should be attached to harnesses to keep any pressure off soft necks and throats. Their main exercise should come from self-directed play in the home or yard. Gentle hills in your yard or play area can help build muscles and stamina. Low lying logs or rocks that require climbing over can help develop coordination.

This should all be facilitated by your puppy's desire to move around in his environment. Rolling a toy along the ground for him to chase after, rather than throwing it far away is a much safer way to play. You can add low obstacles to your puppy's play space as well to encourage building coordination and muscle tone.

Puppies 12 weeks to about 5 months can begin to take slightly longer leash walks, still attached to a harness, but no more than a block or so. If at any time your pup gives up, you know you've likely walked too far. Puppies this age can do some easy exploring in the woods, no lengthy or steep hiking yet though. Allow them to direct their investigations of the new environment. Allow them to climb rocks or logs that are not too high off the ground. Swimming or wading in water to play is a great low stress way to build muscle and coordination.

> For more information on specific exercise see the Resources section

Building a Lasting Bond With Your Puppy Through Play

Building a great relationship with your puppy is so important to making sure you are seen as a safe, trusted and fun person to be around. The easiest and fastest way to build this relationship is with food and play. Everyone in your family should have some involvement —age appropriate —in these aspects of your puppy's life. Everyone that can, should have an opportunity to feed your puppy his meals or treats and everyone should engage in safe and appropriate play with your puppy.

The training exercises outlined in this book allow for plenty of feeding and trust building opportunities. Play is a bit more flexible and subjective depending on your puppy. All the training exercises can and should be treated as games, learning happens so much better when things are made fun. Here are some other games you can play with your puppy that will complement the work you are doing but also help build your relationship.

Tug

Knowing what you now know of your puppy's developing body, it is important to make sure tug is done in a way that does not cause any damage to growing bones, joints, ligaments and muscles. The rule of playing tug with a puppy is that you act as simply an anchor for your puppy to tug a toy against. You should not do any shaking or lifting or swinging with the toy. There can be slight pull back, but it should be gentle and steady not quick and jarring. Let your puppy do the work.

The beauty of tug is it's only fun when you are included, so it lends itself really well to building your relationship. One side benefit of tug is it can help with your puppy learning self-control. The game only happens if he isn't biting at you or jumping on you or otherwise demanding to play. As your puppy gets older, he can also be taught to drop the toy on cue to allow you to throw it or create a game of "drop it, get it."

Tug can help teach mouth control. This is especially good for puppies that don't have a great mastery of their mouthing behavior. Teaching them through play that they need to keep to their side of the toy or the game ends, is pretty powerful stuff for a puppy, no punishment is needed. If teeth touch skin the toy is dropped and the game ends, wait until they have gotten themselves a little calmer and then try the game again. Repeat this process as needed. Also make sure the toy being used is the appropriate length to safely accommodate your puppy's mouth and your hands. Consistency with those rules will teach your puppy how to keep the game going and get you to play with him.

Round Robin Recall

This game is great for the whole family to play. It is a foundational game for coming when called.

With two or more people, everyone loads up with treats or a favored tug toy. Stand at opposite corners of a room and one person at a time calls your puppy's name and then cheerleads him over. Do not use a formal recall word yet. Once your puppy reaches them that person feeds him one treat at a time while praising and gushing over him heavily! Tell your puppy what a smart, wonderful puppy he is while feeding him treat after treat (about 3-5 small pieces) or play tug for a few seconds.

Then, that person stands up and is calm and quiet while the other person performs the same action. Once your puppy gets the game, start moving to other rooms in the house, hiding behind furniture, having each person in separate rooms or playing outside. This is a great game for children to play! This is also an excellent game to play as a substitute for outdoor exercise during inclement weather.

Chase Me

This is another foundational game that helps your puppy keep focus on you and really strengthens the idea that coming to you is super fun and worth their effort.

> *If your puppy gets over excited by this game, make it a little lower key to begin with and gradually increase the excitement level.*
>
> *Jojen gets very barky when we play this game, so I alternate chase with sniffing in the grass for treats and that helps keep the energy level lower.*

Encourage your puppy to chase you by running away while calling his name, when he gets close be evasive and play keep away. Then stand still and let him catch you. Have a ten second party with praise, treats or a toy.

Two Toy Fetch

This is a great interactive game to play with your puppy. Most puppies have an innate chase drive, the tricky part is getting them to pick up the toy and bring it back to you. Don't worry too much about that part of the game in the beginning, getting your puppy to chase after a toy is the first step.

Make the toy that much more enticing by wiggling it around and slightly teasing your puppy with it. Then toss the toy a short distance away. Don't fling it across the yard yet! When your puppy chases after it cheer her on. Have a second toy ready to tease and entice her with and then toss in the other direction. While she's going after the second toy, go grab the first toy and repeat the game. If at any time your puppy picks up the toy or even puts her mouth on it, heap on the verbal praise and encouragement. If she manages to pick it up, you can cheerlead her to you to see if she can carry it all the way. Even if she only carries it a few steps, reward with verbal praise and a toss of the second toy.

Fetch is actually a complex set of behaviors strung together, not every dog —even retrievers believe it or not —will get it right from the beginning. Reward and praise the little steps along the way to the final goal of a complete chase-grab-hold-return behavior sequence.

> *Always remember to make training fun. Using the squeaker of a toy can entice your puppy to be interested in the next toy you toss.*

Henry and Jojen enjoy a game of frisbee

Finn shows his love for tug. This is a great way to combat all the puppy biting. Always have a toy to occupy your puppy's mouth. You can see Finn is starting to lose baby teeth!

Gus enjoying his off-leash training and recall work.

Klaus explores the town

Lady smiling while she practices her off leash skills

Gabby eats her lunch out of a Kong Wobbler

Nusa contemplates the stairs. It's important to make sure you allow your puppy to use stairs slowly to avoid any injuries.

Zelda practicing self-control in front of all the dog toys at the feed store.

Otis Does his best to ignore all the fun toys behind him!

Gus tries out the snufflemat.

CHAPTER 5
Puppies and Kids
How to Live in Peace Together

My daughter Rylie and Beanie watch my husband use the weed trimmer in the yard.

Safety and Management

There are few things more endearing than a child and their puppy. To make sure that they have a wonderful relationship as they both grow it is important to keep safety for both in mind.

The most important aspect when dealing with puppies, and dogs in general, is to have a good understanding of canine body language. It is equally important that all family members respect that communication.

With canine body language, the key is looking at the whole puppy and assess the context the signals are being seen in. A puppy flicking his tongue in and out, may be communicating some stress or nervousness. Or he may simply have some food stuck in his mouth from dinner. Likewise, a puppy growling over a toy could be guarding it or simply "talking" to you to illicit play. In both cases, just looking at one signal alone won't give you the whole picture. Of course, if you are ever unsure of what your puppy is trying to communicate, err on the side of caution and seek the help of a certified trainer.

When I talk about respecting your puppy's body language signals, what I mean is you take a step back —literally and figuratively. Keep yourself safe and try to assess what the situation was that caused the distress in your puppy. The more information you have the better you can be prepared to help teach your puppy to be more comfortable.

These are some common signs of discomfort, worry or stress. Remember, read the whole puppy.

Lip Licking—Their tongue flicks out repeatedly.

Turning head or body away—A puppy may turn their head to the side, up, down or completely away from you.

"Guilty look"—This is deceptive, it is not actually guilt your puppy is exhibiting, it is concern over your behavior, tone of voice or posture.

Paw lift—One of the front paws held up and close to the body. This is often seen in small breed puppies.

Shivering—Even when the weather is warm, or he is inside.

Yawning—Repeated yawning can signal stress.

Body shake off—Shaking off the whole body either during or after an event or interaction. This is a sign of a puppy trying to release stress.

"Whale Eye"—Seeing the whites of your puppy's eyes or when your puppy looks at you out of the corner of his eye. This can be harder to discern in puppies with large buggy eyes, but it is possible to see it.

Freezing—This looks like a puppy with a closed mouth, still body posture, tail either up or down and not moving and breathing is almost imperceptible. This is a very concerning signal and needs to be respected immediately. Move away from the puppy and then get help from your trainer. It can be a pre-cursor to a snap or bite.

Excessive face licking (puppy to human)-This is a context-based behavior. Puppies love to lick our faces, but if yours does so vigorously when you put your face or body close to them, it is likely a sign that they need space. This is seen a lot with toddlers and puppies. The puppy is trying to create some space between them, respect this signal.

Growling—Again this is a more context-based behavior. If your puppy is growling while he plays tug with you or another puppy or even with a toy by himself, it is likely just "talking". If the growling is combined with any of the other listed behaviors and happens around food, toys, people, beds or doorways. This is a concerning behavior and should be respected and addressed by a certified trainer. Never punish a growl! Doing so gets rid of your puppy's early communication sign that he is uncomfortable. This may cause him to escalate to snap or bite "out of the blue." Be thankful for the growl, respect it and then get help to work on it.

Air snapping/biting—Puppies bite when teething but that type of biting is very different than the type that is trying to communicate distress or fear. This is a clear signal indicating fear or discomfort and should be addressed by a professional trainer.

Excessive ground sniffing—This is a displacement behavior that can indicate stress and can also communicate to other dogs that he poses no threat.

It is a misconception that to grow up into a stable dog, a puppy must learn to deal with all kinds of behavior and handling from children and people.

> There are countless books, charts and videos on all the different body signals puppies and dogs give us to communicate how they are feeling. For more information check out the Resources section.

Think of it this way, do you allow your child, or strangers, to hit, jump on, pinch or pull on you? Do you allow people to touch you while you eat or stick their hands in your food? Do you allow people to take your favorite book or your phone out of your hands for no reason? Your puppy should be given the same consideration that you would expect. Teaching children how to safely interact and love their puppy is what builds a beautiful relationship and helps both grow up to be loving adults.

Here are some basic management steps to follow to make sure everyone is safe and happy.

Children 10 & Under

Active Adult Supervision: An adult should be actively involved in the interaction between child and puppy, whether it's play on the floor with an infant or toddler nearby or training games with an elementary age child, adult participation is imperative. Bites, accidental knocking over or stepping on can all happen in an instant. If an adult is not fully present and involved, these types of incidents are more prevalent and less preventable.

Separation time: Children and puppies both benefit from some quiet alone time. This is especially true when you can't actively supervise them both. Separating them with a baby gate, putting the puppy safely in an exercise pen or crate is the safest option. Making sure that the puppy can't be bothered or poked at through a crate, gate or exercise pen is good for everyone. We all need breaks now and then, it is best to give children and puppies multiple breaks throughout the day before they get tired, cranky and inadvertently hurt one another.

Keep feeding separated: Never allow a child to approach a puppy that is eating, whether he is confined to a crate or pen or not. This is not how to prevent resource guarding it can actually cause it. Adults shouldn't do this either. Similarly, don't allow your puppy to pester your child while they're eating, whether at a table or a highchair. Puppy nails and teeth can be very sharp and can accidentally cause an injury if your puppy tries to grab for food. Crate or leash your puppy to you while your child eats, perhaps use this time to play one of the training exercises outlined in this book.

Keep outdoor play controlled: Don't allow your puppy to chase, jump and nip at your child while they're trying to play. Keep your puppy on a leash and play some foundation training games, this is a great way to increase the challenge in any of the games in this book. If your child wants to play with your puppy it should be a very structured game to keep enthusiasm to a minimum to avoid over excitement and unintentional bites or scratches.

Tweens and Teens

Kids in this age group may want a little more control and independence over their interactions with your puppy. You make the judgement based on your child and your puppy. The rules of respecting communication are the same though, if your puppy is exhibiting signs of discomfort, stop and figure out a different way to interact.

Passive Supervision: This age group should be able to be trusted with a less hands on approach to your supervision. This means you are in the same general area while they are interacting in case they need help or a break from the interaction. Puppies get over stimulated easily and teens love to push the envelope, so make sure you are listening. Stress to your teen your concern if their puppy gets overexcited and the potential for accidental bites or scratches.

Involvement in the training process: This age group can take on some responsibility for the training of their puppy. Things like feedings, walks, and group training classes can all be part of raising their puppy. All of the games, except for the explicit adult only body handling games, can be part of your teens' interaction with your puppy. It will build their relationship into something wonderful and long-lasting.

Teaching your children compassion, respect and gentleness when interacting with their puppy sets everyone up for success as they grow.

Caitie and Henry snuggling appropriately

Caitie and Henry play with a toy together

CHAPTER 6
The Vital Basics

Training for a Happy and Healthy Puppy

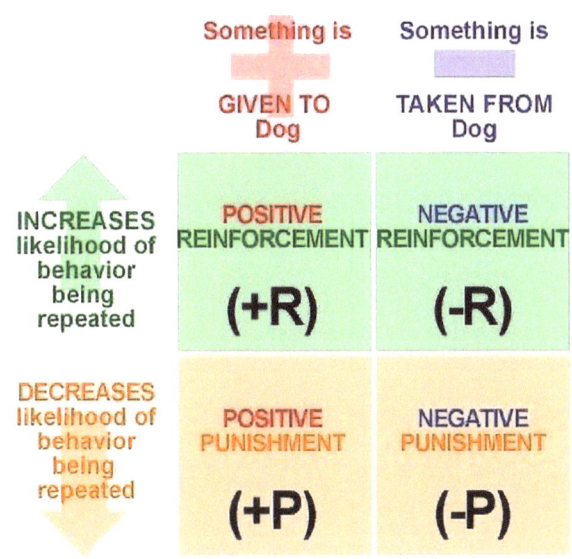

Operant Conditioning Quadrants

Learning Theory and Positive Reinforcement Training (+R)

Understanding the basics of learning theory and positive reinforcement training is the key to understanding how to navigate through your puppy's growth in a way that creates a happy and stable adult dog.

There are four quadrants of training: positive reinforcement, negative reinforcement, positive punishment and negative punishment. These terms can be confusing —even to trainers! The thing to remember is that the term "positive" simply means adding, it does not necessarily mean something that is good or enjoyable. The term "negative" means subtracting or removing. Reinforcement is something that strengthens a behavior. Punishment is something that decreases a behavior.

Positive reinforcement (+R) is the addition of something, like praise, petting or treats, to increase or strengthen a behavior.

Positive punishment (+P) is the addition of something, like a leash correction, verbal correction or shock from a collar, to decrease or stop a behavior.

Negative reinforcement (-R) is the removal of something, such as a sustained shock or an ear pinch, to increase or strengthen a behavior.

Negative punishment (-P) is the removal of something, like the ability to get a treat, your attention, a toy or access to play, to decrease or stop a behavior.

It is important to understand that ALL mammals learn the same way. Your puppy, a dolphin, and you, all learn through the same process. We use the A, B, C method that refers to:

A: Antecedent, or the environment or situation.

B: Behavior, or the action done by the animal.

C: Consequence, or what happened as a result of that behavior or action.

As an example, you are at home (**A**). Your puppy wanders over and picks up his chew bone, lies down to chew it (**B**). You see this and think what a smart little puppy he is, so you walk over, praise him and drop a little treat in front of him (**C**).

Your puppy was just taught that the behavior of picking up his chew bone and chewing on it not only feels good to his teething mouth, but also earns him your attention and a treat. This is pretty powerful stuff. This is positive reinforcement training. In the above example, it is far more likely that puppy will chew on his bone again in that environment because of the addition of the reward, thus creating a stronger behavior.

The exercises in this book use positive reinforcement training. I believe it is the best and most humane way to train our loving companions. It is important to note that the other methods described in the quadrants above also work. However, I feel they are not necessary in teaching your puppy all he needs to learn.

Positive reinforcement training builds trust and confidence in your puppy. It does not diminish your relationship by adding fear and discomfort into the training process. Using positive reinforcement training ensures your puppy enjoys learning from you rather than fearing the consequences if he gets it wrong.

Positive Reinforcement training is built on three elements: management, relationship and communication.

1. Good management sets the dog up for success. This can include properly restricting parts of the house, a daily feeding schedule, adequate exercise and mental stimulation. Start with a good management system from the beginning and you will both be happier!

2. Your relationship with your puppy needs to be built on trust. Having a puppy that is afraid of you is tantamount to disaster. It works against your desire to have your puppy follow your rules. You need to be clear with your puppy about what the boundaries are and do so in a positive manner that helps him learn and trust you.

3. Communication means you both learn to properly listen and understand each other. A good trainer can help that communication along by helping you be precise and consistent with your cues and rules. Your trainer can help you get an idea of what your puppy is trying to tell you when they do certain things or act certain ways. Dogs are all about body language, so it is vital yours is non—threatening as well as clear and concise.

Socialization: Preparing your puppy for the world

Socialization is something most everyone has heard about. You probably know it is important, but what is it exactly? Socialization is not just a matter of taking your puppy to the dog park or letting her meet your neighbors. It is a systematic and deliberate strategy to positively expose your puppy to the experiences and things she will be expected to encounter throughout her life.

> Some breeders and rescues don't allow puppies to go home until 12 weeks, don't worry! If you are happy with your breeder's socialization program or the socialization your puppy got in foster care you are still on a great path. You can still implement all these elements into your socialization plan with your puppy. If you don't know your puppy's socialization background just start from square one and work on catching up!

It is a matter of quality NOT quantity. The critical socialization window for puppies is between 4-12 weeks of age. Your puppy shouldn't come to you before 8 weeks, so you have only a few weeks to work within this developmental period. Don't panic! These charts are designed to help you make a plan for each week of this critical period. It is highly advisable to repeat exposures every week – and more than once—within the time frame.

Animals and Pets

Socialization to other animals —not just other dogs —is important in helping your puppy be comfortable in a variety of settings, such as vet clinics, farms, pet stores, friends' homes and even your daily walks. It is not just enough to socialize your pup with the animals living in your home, although that is a good place to start. Exposing your puppy to your neighbor's chickens, your mother's cat or the horses and sheep at the farm down the road are all part of the process. The most important thing to remember is that every new animal your puppy is exposed to, even if just viewing it from a distance, is paired with something especially wonderful for your puppy.

Seeing a horse from a safe distance = yummy chicken. This is how you help your puppy have good feelings about new and strange animals in the environment. They predict good things for him.

Fill out this chart to track your progress

Age	8 weeks	9 weeks	10 weeks	11 weeks	12 weeks
Kittens					
Puppies					
Adult dogs					
Senior dogs					
Fish tank					
House birds					
Outside birds					
Squirrels					
Chickens					
Ducks/ geese					
Reptiles					
Cows					
Horses					
Pigs					
Donkeys					
Rabbits					
Guinea pigs					
Hamsters					

Example: Bodie the puppy is going to live with a family that owns horses. Bodie needs to be comfortable around them for safety reasons as well as family harmony. Bodie's owner takes him on leash to see the horses from a distance while they are in their field. While Bodie and his owner watch the horses go about their business, Bodie earns his breakfast from his owner, just for seeing these big, strange animals. Doing this at least once a day will teach Bodie that seeing the horses means he gets yummy treats. Bodie starts to love horses!

People

Having your puppy meet many different types of people during this critical socialization period is also important. A puppy that has been exposed to different people will have less fear and challenges with strangers than a puppy that only interacted with immediate family members during this crucial time.

The rule of thumb is your puppy should meet 100 different people by the time he's 12 weeks old. Remember though, that quality, not quantity is your goal. Taking him to a playground and letting him a group of children surround him is the opposite of a quality socialization encounter!

The subject may be different, but the process is the same, pair new people with something yummy or a favorite toy to create a positive association. You might think it's a good idea to let people give your puppy treats, but I don't recommend this. You don't want your puppy to be fearful of seeing and potentially meeting new people, but you also don't want him thinking all strangers carry food. That will make your attention training more challenging. All the treats should come from you as a reward for a nice interaction or for simply seeing people from afar. Here is a simple chart of the types of people your puppy should meet.

Fill out this chart to track your progress

Age	8 weeks	9 weeks	10 weeks	11 weeks	12 weeks
Babies					
Toddlers					
School age children					
Teenagers					
Adults					
Multi cultural/ ethnicities					
People in wheelchairs					
Elderly people					
People with walkers					
Tall people					
Short people					
Large people					
Uniformed police officers					
Uniformed Fire fighter					
UPS driver					
Mailman					
Veterinarian					
People in hats					
People with beards					
People in big jackets					

Example: Sadie is going to live with a family that has a police officer friend. Sadie and her owners go to visit their friend at the station and bring really yummy treats. The uniformed police officer allows Sadie to approach on her own and when she does, the officer doesn't crowd her. Sadie then earns a treat from her owner, thus feeling comfortable with the police officer. Sadie gets braver and initiates attention from the police officer and can begin to associate a person dressed like that as a good thing.

Surfaces, Places, Sounds and Things

In your puppy's lifetime he will visit many places, be exposed to different sounds, walk on different surfaces and see unusual things in his environment. The best way to make sure he is comfortable with all of it is to do the work while he's young and positively expose him to as much as possible.

Surfaces

Walking your puppy on different surfaces may seem like an easy thing to deal with, but you would be surprised how many dogs show a very real preference for surfaces, both for walking on and potty preferences. It can even affect how they move about in the home. Getting your puppy comfortable with all of it will make travel so much easier. A puppy that has learned that it is okay to potty outside on concrete is an easy traveling companion.

Fill out this chart to track your puppy's progress

Age	8 weeks	9 weeks	10 weeks	11 weeks	12 weeks
Bark mulch					
Stone					
Concrete					
Grass/wet grass					
Artificial grass/ scratchy rugs					
Sand					

Mossy undergrowth					
Blacktop					
Hard wood floors					
Ceramic tile floors					
Linoleum floors					

Example: Kodee goes home to his new family when there is still snow on the ground. His owner knows spring is coming so she finds a patch of grass in the yard for Kodee to explore. Kodee's owner knows to utilize her puppy's love of using his nose to help facilitate the new surface introduction. She drops a small handful of his breakfast in the grass and lets Kodee wander around finding all the treats. This helps Kodee interact with the new surface in a very reinforcing way. She can also feed him treats directly from her hand as he wanders around the grass.

Places

The best way to get your puppy comfortable in all the places she may visit in her life is to positively expose her to them during this early developmental stage. Pair each new place with treats and/or play to help associate good feelings with the environment. Fill in this chart to track your progress

Age	8 weeks	9 weeks	10 weeks	11 weeks	12 weeks
Veterinary office					
Police station					
Fire station					
Post Office					
Town Offices					
School					
Playground					
Shopping center					

Pet store					
Grooming Salon					
Training centers					

Example: Casey's new family knows she will need to see the veterinarian on a regular basis to stay healthy. They make a plan to visit the vet office as often as possible just for a "happy visit" before Casey even needs to be seen for her vaccines. Casey visits with the staff and receives some treats for meeting new people and being in a new place. Casey's owner lets her explore the space, earn yummy treats and maybe play a little game of tug, then they leave to go home. A short, sweet visit means Casey will be much happier to visit the next time she has an appointment. Casey's vet is happy too, it makes her job so much easier!

Sounds

Sound phobias can be very real and very damaging. Getting your puppy accustomed to the regular sounds of your home as well as any outdoor and nature sounds is vital to their mental health as they mature.

Fill in this chart to track your puppy's progress

Age	8 weeks	9 weeks	10 weeks	11 weeks	12 weeks
Thunder					
High winds					
Blender					
Smoke alarm					
Phone ringing					
Doorbell					
Door knocking					
Baby crying					

Dogs barking					
School bus					
Lawn Mower					
Hair dryer					
Vacuum cleaner					
Motorcycle					
Sirens					
Dryer/washing machine					
Dishwasher					

Example: Jack's owners know that soon they would also like to add a human baby to their family, so to prepare Jack they use a sound app to start the process of familiarizing Jack with the sounds of a baby crying while he eats yummy stuff or plays a game with his owners. Jack's owners start with the sound barely audible and carefully increase the volume over time, all the while pairing the sound with food or play.

> A great tool for sound training is the Sound Proof Puppy Training app. It is available for Apple and Android devices.

Novel Items

Anything new in your puppy's environment has the potential to cause a fear-based reaction. Trash cans, cardboard boxes, holiday decor, ceiling fans or balloons can all be scary to a small puppy. Pair yummy treats with any new thing your puppy encounters to help build their resiliency and confidence to explore their world.

Fill out this chart to track your puppy's progress

Age	8 weeks	9 weeks	10 weeks	11 weeks	12 weeks
Trash Cans					
Cardboard boxes					
Broom					
Vacuum cleaner					
Revolving doors					
Elevators					
Garage doors					
Lawn mower					
Crate					
Baby gates					
School bus					
Garbage/delivery truck					
Construction equipment					
Baby Strollers					
Wheelchairs					
Medical equipment					
Bicycles					
Motorcycles					
Skis					
Snowmobile					
Sled					
Skateboard					

Example: Bandit's family knows that they will need to be able to clean their home, especially with a puppy around. To make sure the vacuum cleaner doesn't scare him, Bandit's family takes the vacuum out and just lets it rest near the wall for a few days. His owner tosses treats around the vacuum and praises and rewards any investigation of the machine as it sits there. Soon, Bandit doesn't see the vacuum as a potentially scary thing. His owner then begins to move the vacuum around, all while tossing treats to Bandit as the vacuum moves. Then, they turn the vacuum on once Bandit is no longer concerned with the motion of the vacuum cleaner. This process makes Bandit more comfortable with the loud moving machine and makes cleaning the house much easier for his owner.

Training

Positive reinforcement training is about teaching your puppy what behavior you want him to do instead, rather than punishing the behavior you don't like. An example is a puppy that likes to jump. Instead of jumping you might want him to sit. Sit can be taught to replace the jumping behavior. Your puppy can't be jumping if he's sitting and if sitting gets him what he wants. This is most likely your attention. He is far more likely to sit than jump – as long as the sit, not the jumping, gets him what he wants!

To help your puppy grasp this concept faster, we use a marker word like, "yes" or "good." This word is used when your puppy performs the behavior we like and tells him he is about to be rewarded in some way. The sequence would go like this: You cue "sit," your puppy sits, you say "yes" and then reward your puppy. Marker words should be short and succinct to get the information to your puppy quicker and allow for quicker reward delivery. Too much verbal chatter can really muddy the training process. Remember, they don't actually speak our language, we need to be clear and concise in our communication. Don't get bogged down in monologues!

There is also a difference in how you can reward your puppy for a behavior. You can simply do a 1:1 ratio; 1 cookie for 1 behavior like, a sit or a down. You can also give a jackpot reward that is at least 5 cookies doled out one at a time. This type of reward is used for really difficult behaviors like recall, attention away from distraction, potty training, crate training or anytime your puppy does something amazing!

Speaking of treats, positive reinforcement training uses a LOT of treats. To make sure you don't overfeed your puppy or create and upset stomach, use his kibble for most training sessions. As long as your puppy really likes his kibble it is a great way to train and make sure he isn't getting too many extras. For things like potty training, having kibble near the door he goes out of will make rewarding easier. You can also split his daily ration of food into smaller portions for training opportunities throughout the day. This ensures your puppy still gets the required amount of food, but it is used as efficiently as possible for training purposes.

Positive reinforcement training also calls for using higher value rewards for more difficult behaviors, like recall and attention around distractions. Foods like string cheese, boiled chicken or turkey are great. Be careful of many store-bought treats that are high in sugar. Freeze dried meat treats are also a great option as they don't go bad if accidentally left in a coat pocket! You want treats to be small, soft and easily consumable rather than large or crunchy.

Having treats ready throughout your home and on walks make training much easier and progress much faster. I like to keep little containers of kibble and dried treats all around the area my puppy spends most of his time, so I am able to reward any behavior I see, quickly, to ensure that behavior gets stronger. I always have a treat pouch ready for going outside for walks or play so I can be ready when my puppy decides to come when I call instead of chasing the neighbors' cat!

Here is how we deal with a behavior we don't like using positive reinforcement training:

Interrupt: use the name game, positive interrupter noise, hand clap or whistle

Divert: redirect your puppy to acceptable chew toy, cue like sit, outside potty spot

> My favorite training treats are sample bags of different kibble from any pet store, Nature's Variety Raw Bites, Pure Bites freeze dried meat treats, Zukes training treats and Wellness Jerky bites.

Praise: use your voice or a marker word, like yes, good or right

Reward: use verbal praise paired with food treats, petting, toys or games

When you see your puppy being good, make sure to reward!

Potty Training

The basic rules of potty training are consistency and management. Consistency means taking your puppy out the same door to potty every single time. This will create a pattern that will eventually lead to your puppy giving you the cue that she needs to go outside by going to that door and barking or scratching or simply sitting and waiting. Feeding schedules should be regular and consistent as well. A puppy that eats all day long has a much less predictable potty schedule. Consistency is also taking your puppy out on a regular schedule, at least every hour and definitely after napping, playing, eating or drinking. Set an alarm clock, kitchen timer or the timer on your phone to help remind you.

Management means you set up your puppy's environment in such a way that mistakes are as minimal as possible and easy to clean up when they do happen. Management means limiting access within the house to the room or two that you spend most of your day in. A puppy allowed to roam the entire house is one that will develop some very strong, undesirable indoor bathroom habits. A good rule of thumb is if you can't watch your puppy closely, like when you need to shower, make a meal, or leave the house for any reason, then she should be crated, leashed to you or otherwise confined to a small puppy proofed area like an exercise pen in the house. When you do need to confine your puppy make sure they have eliminated recently and have access to appropriate chew toys for unsupervised play.

Life doesn't stop when you get a puppy. Wouldn't it be nice if it did? My favorite way to go about my daily activities at home is by tethering my puppy to my waist with a leash. This allows me to discern my puppy's potty signals. It also gives me an easy opportunity to work on training exercises.

Your puppy may have very clear potty signs, or they may be very subtle. Some things to watch for are excessive sniffing, circling, wandering away, jumping on you, whining or barking. The signs given may afford you plenty of time to get your puppy out or they may be simultaneous. This is why it is important to keep such a close eye on your puppy, to help eliminate any mistakes in this process.

When you do take your puppy outside to potty, make sure it is on leash. If you want her to potty in the same spot, then you need to go to that spot immediately, be as boring as possible acting as an anchor. Let her sniff and wander only as far as her leash will allow until she has eliminated. Be patient, puppies are notorious for not fully eliminating and then doing so once they get back inside. Once she has gone potty then you can let her wander the yard to sniff —great socialization and mental stimulation. Don't immediately go in to the house after she eliminates. Doing so can create a puppy that holds it while outside because they want to prolong their time outside and they've learned once they potty they go right back inside. Give her time to see if she has more to do and then you can feel safe bringing her in until the timer goes off in an hour for her next trip out.

Sometimes puppies get so distracted by the outdoors they "forget" to potty. Don't get frustrated, if she doesn't go in the first 5-10 minutes, take her back in, but watch her closely and take her back out 2-5 minutes later to try again. Don't assume she doesn't have to go! You may have to repeat this pattern a few times. Just be patient and consistent, and you will avoid any mistakes. When your puppy does eliminate outside, heap on the verbal praise and if you have cookies on you —which you should —dole out 3-5, one at a time, all while praising her. Eliminating outside pays BIG dividends!

When your puppy does have an accident inside, DO NOT punish her. If you can interrupt the flow and quickly get her outside to allow her to finish, great. If you miss it, you just need to clean it thoroughly with an enzyme cleaner and make sure you are more vigilant next time. Your puppy is not being spiteful or stubborn by eliminating in the house, you just weren't watching her closely enough to see her signals or you missed the alarm to take her out. Punishing bodily functions only serves to make your puppy wary of eliminating in front of you, causing frustration and more indoor accidents.

Crate Training

Having a puppy that is comfortable and happy in a crate makes everyone's life so much easier. Crates allow puppies a safe place to rest, eat, and chew on bones. Crates also allow puppy owners time to make dinner, help the kids with homework, do the dishes, take a shower or go grocery shopping without worrying that your puppy is getting into things he shouldn't or wrecking any potty-training progress.

The set-up of your puppy's crate is very important. You want to make sure it is in a relatively quiet area, but not isolated from the family. Some families have two crates, one for daytime use and one for bedtime in another room in the house. If you just have one, make sure its location is convenient for you to use throughout the day.

When your puppy is in his crate it should be considered a safe space. He shouldn't be subjected to teasing or fingers poking in at him. He should be left with an appropriate crate toy and comfy bedding —unless he shreds or eats bedding —and given time to relax, sleep or eat in peace.

Here are some ways to get your puppy comfortable in the crate:

Feed your puppy in his crate for every meal.

Randomly sprinkle treats in his crate to be discovered throughout the day.

Play crate games

Crate Game 1:

1. Toss a cookie into the back of your puppy's crate. Allow him to go in and get it and turn around facing the door.

2. Before he can come out begin feeding him treats one at a time in rapid succession, essentially keeping him in his crate.

After about 5-10 treats inside the crate, toss a treat for him to come out of the crate and retrieve.

1. Repeat this process a handful of times. Remember, when he is in the crate, he gets a jackpot of treats as well as plenty of verbal praise.

Once your puppy understands the first game you can change it up a little.

Crate Game 2:

1. Toss a cookie into the back of your puppy's crate. Allow him to go in and get it and turn around facing the door.

2. Feed your puppy his jackpot reward, then toss a cookie out for him to go get.

3. Stare at the crate – not your puppy – and see if he makes any connection between the crate and the reward.

4. You can use your marker word for behavior that engages the crate in anyway. A look, nose sniff, one foot in, leaning in, getting the front part of his body in or all of his body in are all rewardable behaviors. You can toss his reward for the behavior INTO the crate, feed a jackpot reward and then start over again.

The lightbulb should go on quickly and the connect between the jackpot reward and the crate will begin to form. Your puppy should start voluntarily going into his crate for his jackpot reward. Make sure to verbally praise him as well.

> For further information and to see how these ideas are carried out, see the videos posted on the Wicked Good Dog Training YouTube channel

Soft Mouth Foundation Training

A teething puppy can be a real pain! It is an important part of development that your puppy learns bite inhibition, or how hard is too hard to use his mouth. The rule to remember, and to make sure EVERYONE that interacts with your puppy follows, is that hands are not toys. Rough housing or playing with your puppy using your hands encourages biting behavior and does the opposite of teaching a gentle mouth. Playing this way with your puppy may be fine for you, but your elderly parent or small child may not appreciate it and a puppy is still too young and untrained yet to know the difference.

If you are already aware of how hard your puppy bites during play, you can skip this exercise and move to exercise #2. But if you are still trying to judge your puppy's mouth pressure you can try this. This is just an assessment tool. Hopefully your puppy learned from his litter mates and mother how hard is too hard to bite. These are Adult only exercises.

Exercise 1: Holding your hands still, allow your puppy to mouth at your hands. You can judge pretty quickly how much pressure your puppy is using. If it is consistently hard and painful, or if your puppy gets overly excited by mouthing your hands, discontinue the exercise and move to exercise #2.

If the pressure is minimal praise your puppy and offer a dropped treat. If at times the pressure increases calmly say "ouch" and remove your hand. No need to scold or yell, it should be just enough to let your puppy take a break and look at you, when he does, drop another treat. Continue the exercise only long enough to assess your puppy's ability to inhibit his bite pressure consistently. This exercise should last no more than 1-2 minutes and be done at a time when your puppy is relatively calm and has recently eaten.

Once you have established your puppy's bite inhibition, it is time to improve it or make sure it stays gentle.

> If at any time your "ouch" elicits a greater urgency in your puppy to bite harder or he gets more excited by it, discontinue the exercise and let your trainer know.

Exercise 2: For one of your puppy's meals, whichever you have the most free time for, sit down either on the floor or in a chair with his food bowl. Take one small handful out at a time and in a closed fist offer it to your puppy. They are probably going to mug your hand and chew on it. If teeth touch your skin, even if it doesn't hurt, say "ouch" and remove your hand, count to three and then offer your hand again. You may need to repeat this process a few times before the puppy "gets it."

What you are striving for is that when you offer your hand your puppy licks it gently or nudges it softly with his nose. When he does this open your palm and let him eat the food inside. Once your puppy is reliably licking or nudging your hand every time you offer it, start pairing the command "gentle," "easy," "nice" or whatever command you want to use, when you offer your hand. Don't forget verbal praise too! This exercise can be done when playing with toys together too.

All other play with a teething puppy should always involve a toy of some kind. My favorite is a rope toy that is long enough to accommodate the puppy's mouth and my hand without an accidental meeting of the two. Consistency is key, teach your puppy what the appropriate toy is by continually presenting it to him to occupy his busy mouth.

Remember: **HANDS ARE NOT TOYS!**

Henry gets a ride in a puppy stroller, allowing him to experience a bookstore from a less vulnerable position on the floor. Small puppies can get easily overwhelmed when down low. Allowing them to ride in a stroller or cart can help.

Ica visits the local garden and feed store

Klaus takes his time trying to figure out this water thing. He eventually loved it! The first Siberian I've ever met that loves to swim. Allowing your puppy to make the choice, rather than forcing him in the water, makes all the difference to their confidence.

Otis watches the world go by while we eat ice cream on the patio

Gabby explores walking on a different surface, rocks!

Gabby demonstrates riding in a cart in a store. It's safe for her and she still gets the important socialization.

Caring for The Whole Puppy

Henry meets Thurber and asks to be friends

Gus checks out some playground equipment. Playgrounds are great places to get your puppy comfortable with sounds and motion.

Henry explores neighborhood statuary

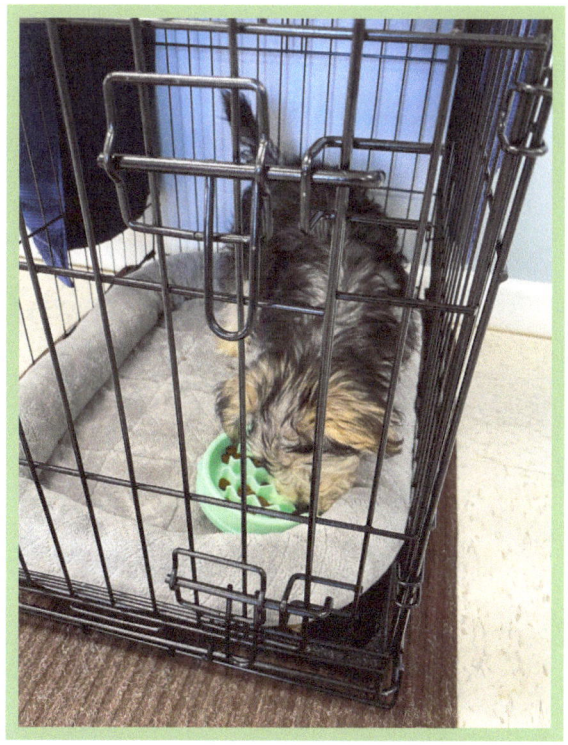

Lunch is served in a slow feeder in the crate

Ica learning that a crate is a great place for a nap. No need to close the door, let your puppy choose to come in and out of their crate as they wish throughout the day.

Caring for The Whole Puppy   75

Beanie meets our cat Boris

Puppies explore novel objects in a class

Beanie gets to meet some mini horses at the local farm. Notice his posture is a little back leaning, he's a little unsure here.

In this picture Beanie has decided the horses aren't scary after all, and readily walked up to investigate.

Finn plays tug with his mom. Tug is a great outlet for puppy energy.

Finn explores some agility equipment, preparing for the future!

Finn checks out the bridge to cross. As always let your puppy make the choice to explore safely.

Gabby learns she can potty on a grass strip in a parking lot! This behavior can be so important when traveling with your dog.

Jojen meets Beanie. When there is such a large size difference between dogs it's important that play is closely supervised, and excitement is kept to a minimum to avoid any accidental injury or scaring of the puppy.

Abby relaxing and being adorable!

Evie showing off excellent attention

Caring for The Whole Puppy   79

Percy and I explore one of the local park areas

Marlo works on her sit while there is big road equipment nearby.

Zoe practices her sit in the local stationary store

CHAPTER 7
Foundation Training Games
Skill Building Fun

Oakley practices being on strange surfaces

Teaching foundational exercises is important for building strong behaviors as your puppy grows. Teaching these exercises in the form of a game makes it much more fun for you and your puppy. Training is a serious, vital business, but it should absolutely be fun! Strong behaviors are born from a strong foundation. These games all work on the basic foundations for attention, leash skills, coming when called, resource guarding prevention and body handling

The Name Game

Most people think teaching their puppy the basics of sit, down and stay are the most important behaviors. I would strongly disagree! The most important behavior to teach your puppy is attention to you. You can't ask your puppy to follow any cues if he has no desire to pay attention to you. Teaching attention can be accomplished a few ways, but my favorite, and how I train every single client I work with regardless of their challenges, is with the Name Game. The object of this game is to teach a strong positive association with his name so that you can easily get your puppy's attention from anything.

This game teaches your puppy that his name means something special. It means he is about to earn some kind of food reward from you when he hears it. If done well and consistently this can be your most powerful tool as your puppy grows to adulthood.

How to Play:

1. Start with a small handful of your puppy's breakfast, standing in front of your puppy, say his name, feed him a treat. At this point all that is happening is he hears his name and is fed a piece of food.

    Repeat this until the handful of food is gone; you are starting to make the association between his name and food.

    Let him finish his meal as normal. Repeat the same process at lunch and dinner.

2. Throughout the day, if you have a toy or treat in your hand or nearby, say your puppy's name then deliver the treat, toss the toy or play a game of tug. Build that association!

    After a couple days playing the game at this level, you can start to change it and increase the challenge.

3. With a small handful of your puppy's meal, play the first version for 5 repetitions, then on the 6th repetition toss the

treat a short distance away. While he's eating the treat and looking away from you, say his name loudly and clearly. Say it only once! As soon as he turns his head back towards you, use your marker word, yes or good, and then toss a piece of food in a different direction. Repeat this process until your handful of food is gone. Feed the rest of your puppy's meal as normal.

4. Play this version randomly throughout the day, any time your puppy is distracted or about to get into mischief. Understand that you have to have something to reward him with when he complies, even if it means you just get on the floor for him to play with. Name response has to always be followed by something good in these early learning stages to really build a strong association and an automatic reaction.

5. Play this game using a novel sound as well, such as a whistle or kissy noise. Go through all the steps from the beginning, just replacing your puppy's name with the sound you have chosen.

This game builds the foundation for all other learned behaviors. It has to be rock solid, so even if you say his name in frustration because he just knocked over your plant, if he looks at you he needs to be rewarded for that. Don't worry you are NOT rewarding the naughty behavior; it will have passed too quickly in his mind to build that association. If your puppy only has intermittent attention to you, further training will be much more difficult and frustrating as he grows. Do the work now to reap the benefits later. Play this game anywhere and everywhere, as often as you can!

> I love playing this game with my dogs. I still play it with Jojen and Sadie and they are 8! It's a game to play throughout your puppy's life.

The Automatic Check In

This game requires more patience and silence on your part. It is all about letting your puppy think and figure things out. We all want our puppies to grow up trusting us and looking to us for direction. This game instills in your puppy that, in the absence of any other information, the best thing to do is look at you or check in with you. It requires your patience because this is not a cued behavior. It is a behavior you want your puppy to offer on his own. My favorite place to work on this is outside in the yard or on a walk.

1. Make sure you have a pocketful of treats or kibble.

2. Anytime your puppy looks up or back at you, use your marker word and drop a treat by your side.

3. Play this game inside and outside. Reward your puppy anytime they lay eyes on you. Remember, you can reward with verbal praise, food or play, use what you have available to you.

Follow Me

This leash skills foundation game will get your puppy primed for real life leash skills anywhere you take her. Because young puppy's bones, joints and ligaments are still soft and delicate it is important not to go for long leash walks or hikes. This game is best done off leash in your home or fenced back yard, so there is no possibility of leash pulling and unintended injuries. Another benefit of this game is to help change the behavior of puppies that like to bite ankles and pant legs.

1. Have treats in both hands, play in a low distraction area.

2. Move around the environment and drop a treat from the hand on whichever side she is on. Allow her to chew and then move on. You can give verbal encouragement to follow you, but this is NOT coming when called so refrain from using "come." Cues like "let's go", "with me", "heel", "follow", etc. are all acceptable encouraging phrases.

3. When she is reliably following you everywhere, start to make it a bit more challenging by randomly changing direction or pace. This makes her have to really pay attention to keep up with you and stay close to earn those treats.

4. When your puppy really begins to understand the game, add the leash. You can let her drag it at first and then alternate between holding it and playing and dropping it and playing. You want your puppy to be able to play this game whether the leash is attached or not.

5. Take this game everywhere! Play in your home, your backyard, a friend's house, the pet store, the vet office, etc.

> When Jojen was little he had the bad habit of walking right behind my feet. It made it difficult to not accidentally kick him as I walked. We played this game a lot to really teach him where the treats happen. He was walking next to me in no time. This will also help with those puppies that like to surge ahead!

Catch Me If You Can

This recall foundation game can lead to a behavior that may one day save your dogs' life. Coming when called is one of the most important behaviors your puppy can learn. If your puppy has a strong foundation of being rewarded for coming to you, it can mean so much more freedom as he grows up and give you a greater sense of security.

It is important to note that any chase type game should always be your puppy chasing you, not the other way around. Chasing your puppy creates a dog that finds running away from you highly reinforcing and will make your recall work so much harder.

1. In a low distraction area, armed with toys or treats, call your puppy's name and make encouraging sounds. Don't use a formal command yet. Back away from your puppy enticing them to run toward you. When she catches you, she gets a little

5-10 second party of verbal praise, petting, toy playing and treats. Whatever she finds fun is what happens when she reaches you.

2. Repeat this game randomly throughout the day. As she gets proficient in this game increase the challenge, move away faster, change direction, hide behind obstacles etc. Only challenge your puppy as much as she is willing to work with. If hiding causes her to lose interest and wander off, hold off on that challenge for a while. You want her super motivated to get to you every time.

3. Play this game everywhere and anywhere, even on leash! You are building a strong foundation behavior that can withstand any challenge. Invest the time and energy now to reap the benefits later.

> Sadie loved to play this game when she was little. She was always so good at catching me, I could never outrun her. To this day, it's her favorite game to play!

Gotcha Game

Some of the biggest and often most dangerous complaints I get for adolescent or adult dogs is that they do not tolerate their collars being touched. Some dogs will even bite to demonstrate their deep distrust and dislike of this type of body handling. Having a dog that is averse to having their collar touched can be difficult for leash walking and grooming among other things.

Teaching your puppy at this early stage that hands coming toward his head and touching or grabbing his collar is not a bad or scary thing can help stave off issues later on with this type of body handling.

This game is intended to condition your puppy to be comfortable with having his collar touched and/or grabbed. This skill is for emergency purposes and leashing ease. Grabbing your puppy's collar is not an acceptable way to move him or handle him on a regular basis.

Step 1: The goal of this step is to ensure your puppy does not back away or duck his head from an outstretched hand. Armed with a small handful of treats in one hand, reach toward your puppy's head with the other, like you are about to pet him, but you won't actually touch him yet. As long as his head stays relatively still, you can reward him with a treat from the other hand. Repeat this step about 5-6 times, alternating hands, then end the exercise. Work at this step for about a week.

> If your puppy is really sensitive with this step and can't keep their head still, then shorten your reach so you don't come so close to the head. Always go at your puppy's pace, pushing and rushing this exercise can lead to frustration and cause the problem you are trying to prevent.

Step 2: Repeat Step 1 for 3-4 repetitions, then present a treat for him to nibble on as you reach to touch his collar gently, you are not grabbing yet. Repeat this step about 5-6 times, alternating hands, then end the game. Work at this step for about a week.

Step 3: Repeat Step 2 for 3-4 repetitions then, offer the food and touch the collar area *at the same time*. Repeat this step about 5-6 times then quit the game. Work at this step for about a week.

Step 4: Repeat Step 3 for 3-4 repetitions then, reach to touch the collar first then offer the treat, repeat this step about 5-6 times and then quit. Work at this step for about a week.

Step 5: Once your puppy is comfortable at Step 4, it is time to add a little challenge to the exercise. You know your puppy best so start where he will be the most successful and work your way up from there. Always start at Step 1 with any new challenge added.

1. Change where your hand reaches, like over the head, from the side or under the chin.

2. Add a cue to the game like "Gotcha." It is the name of the game, but you can use any cue you want!

3. Increase the speed with which you reach for the collar.

4. Change your reaching position, like instead of being in front of your puppy, stand to the side and reach, stand behind him or stand over him.

5. Combine any of these ideas at one time. Say "Gotcha" as you reach quickly over your puppy's head.

6. Make the grab a little more noticeable. Think of an emergency situation where you would need to grab your puppy quickly. Add in a little of that urgency at a time so the force of an emergency grab isn't so scary in the moment it's needed.

> A few things to remember; stop at any time if your dog gets nervous or objects in any way to this process. Go as slow in this process as your dog needs. Keep sessions short, sweet and only once or twice a day. Start by touching the collar from UNDER the chin and then gradually move to the side of the neck then eventually from over the head. Remember this is not for everyday handling or punishment purposes!

Eye, Ears and Mouths, OH MY!

Being able to handle your puppy's eyes, ears and mouth as she grows is going to be so important to making sure she stays as healthy as possible. Ear infections are painful and cause permanent damage. Tooth and mouth care are vital to the health of your puppy as well. Being able to safely and calmly care for these parts of your puppy will make life so much easier for you, your puppy and your vet! As with any body handling exercise monitor your puppy's body language and make note of any sensitivities or aversions to what you are doing. Then either adjust accordingly or stop altogether so as to not make the situation worse.

Mouth: To start with handling or touching the mouth area, begin by using one or two fingers to slowly stroke his muzzle on top. Move from the tip of his nose to where it meets the skull, and then the sides moving from nose to face, with the grain of hair and whiskers. Be careful not to make the touch too light as it may be ticklish for some puppies. You may not want to use food during this as that can sometimes make things a little less relaxed. However, if your puppy really objects to this, you can add in a little treat to help things along.

Eyes: For the eyes, use the flat of your four fingers and move smoothly from the base of his nose, gently over his eye towards the ear. Again, keep your pressure light, but not ticklish. Be sure to work on each eye, one at a time. Right now, we just want to get your puppy to associate hands on his face as a relaxing exercise.

Ears: For the ears, begin with a cupped hand at the base of the ear and gently move your hand out to the tip of the ear. You can carefully place your thumb in the underside of the ear, so they get the sensation of something inside their ear a bit too. Do not go down the ear canal. Work both ears one at a time.

Tail, Legs and Feet Too

It is important for your puppy to be comfortable with hands on all parts of his body. He may never enjoy it fully but if trained properly he will allow it with as little fuss as possible. Being able to handle your puppy's feet means you can check his pads for scrapes or cuts, trim his nails, or get snowballs out from between his toes. The tail can sometimes be a place where twigs, leaves and bugs may reside, you'll want to be able to work with your puppy's tail to keep him clean. Handling the legs means you can assess an injury, dry him off, or maneuver his legs to get his harness on.

These steps help to make sure you or your vet can have access to all parts of your puppy for examination and any medical or husbandry care that may need to be done. As always, monitor your puppy's body language and reaction to any of these exercises.

Tail: To start with the tail, using a flat palm, you will move your hand down your puppy's back from base of the neck out to the tip of the tail. As you reach the tail cup your hand slightly, so you are gently encircling the tail. Do not grab or try to move, wiggle or lift the tail. You are simply stroking along your puppy's spine. While you do this you can monitor his body condition. Is his spine felt by your hand, is there too thick a layer of fat to feel it, is it too bony, does there seem to be any sensitivity as you travel down the spine? These are some of the things you will be able to discern just from this one body handling exercise and if you have worked this enough with your puppy when he is healthy you will know immediately by touch, if something is wrong.

Legs: Being able to handle your puppy's legs is important as it can help you discern if there is any injury, and where specifically it may be.

Begin by cupping your hand lightly around the top of one leg and gently but firmly move your hand down to the ankle. Do not pick up the leg at this time. You just want to feel the structure of the leg itself in its natural state. If your puppy is lying down for this, be careful not to move his leg at an unnatural angle.

Move on to each other leg. You may find one leg is more sensitive than the others, if you don't think it has to do with pain, just make a mental not of it and break down the handling of that leg into smaller steps. You can just rest a finger on the leg for one second, as long as your puppy does not pull away you can reward with a treat or simply remove your finger. Work at your puppy's pace and be respectful of his body language. A growl is information, don't take it personally and don't discipline it. Your puppy is simply telling you he is not comfortable with that handling yet. Your job is to change how he feels about that by respecting his information and helping him through it with positive associations.

Feet: Working with your puppy's feet is very tricky. It is a rare adult dog that does not have some sensitivity to having their feet handled. This is why it's so important to start now! You need to start slow or you could create bigger problems for yourself and your puppy. Begin by simply lifting and resting your puppy's paw in the palm of your hand. If your puppy is lying down, you can do the same thing. Don't attempt to close your hand or stroke the foot or toes, simply let it rest in your palm. Hold that position for no more than three seconds at a time. If you need to use food to reward or distract, go ahead and do so. Move on to the other three feet and repeat the process. Do the whole process twice and then give your puppy a break from the body handling.

> Remember these are foundational exercises. You will need to keep working on this as your puppy gets older. A good trainer or training class can help you progress this type of body handling further. All Body handling exercises can be seen on the Wicked Good Dog Training YouTube channel.

Resource Guarding Prevention Game or "What Do You Have?"

Resource guarding can be a serious issue. Even if your puppy has not expressed such behavior, we can create issues by our behavior if we aren't careful.

It is very important that your puppy learns early on that when people approach him while he has a toy or food item it is a good thing rather than something to be concerned about. One of the biggest mistakes people make with new puppies is becoming hyper-focused on what is in their mouth. They are constantly grabbing things out of their puppy's mouth, even if it's an innocuous item, like grass or a leaf. There are definitely times when it is prudent to get something dangerous out of your puppy's mouth, but you need to be careful not to be fanatic about it. Doing so can create a puppy that feels threatened every time you come near him when he has something. This can result in your puppy immediately swallowing the item, running away from you with it or acting out by growling or snapping.

To help ensure this does not become the case we can play the prevention game.

Step 1: When your puppy is eating his food, has a food dispensing toy or a chew bone, simply walk by and say, "what do you have?" and then drop a better piece of food by his toy and walk on. You are not reaching for the item, bending down or even stopping. It's a random drive by food drop while he is occupied with something he likes. Don't do this every time he has something, keep it random and sporadic. Play at this level for about a week or so.

Your goal with Step 1 is to get to the point that when you approach him while he has his item, he lifts his head on your approach and begins expecting a treat.

Step 2: When your puppy is fully involved with some prized item or food you will approach, say "what do you have?", reach down and drop your treat then walk on. You are not trying to touch or take the item you are just reaching towards it to drop your treat. Play at this level for a week or so.

> If at any time in this game you see your puppy "freeze" or get very still while hovering over the item or he eats even faster as you approach, stop the game and let your trainer know immediately. Freezing is a sign of actual resource guarding and may be a precursor to a bite or snap. You do not want to push your puppy past that point, so it is important to get help as soon as possible.

Your puppy should be comfortable now with your approach and reach. To continue this game follow Step 3 randomly throughout the next few weeks.

Step 3: When your puppy is involved in something, inside or outside, approach him, say "what do you have?", reach down and touch or slightly lift the item, very briefly, release it and also drop a treat, then walk away.

Training Exercises with Your Puppy and Your Child

Here are some ways to modify some of the training games in this book to include children in the process. Kids love to be helpers. If we give clear and simple instructions, they can be wonderful partners in raising their puppy to be a fantastic dog and companion.

Name Game: Children love playing this game. For the young children, they can drop the treats on the ground when their puppy responds to his name or be the one to call the puppy's name. The safest treat delivery for young children is to have them drop the treats on the ground for their puppy to find. It may make the game a little slower, but it is just as effective. Children over ten can play this game as described, if their puppy is especially rough taking treats, it is always okay to drop the treats on the ground.

Follow Me: This one is easy, simply let your young child walk around the house with you, dropping treats as they go. Let your puppy earn half or all of his meal this way. Playing in the grass in the back yard makes for a slower game but can really challenge your puppy to keep following. The distractions and mental stimulation of searching for food in the grass is a great brain workout for your puppy.

Catch Me: This game can be played by children with active adult supervision. You want to make sure there isn't the possibility of over excitement or getting knocked over. Have your child call their puppy's name then cheer their puppy on to come running to them. Kids generally love to cheer! As their puppy approaches, an adult drops a small handful of treats on the ground in front of the child. As their puppy is eating the child backs up a few steps and repeats the game.

Chase Me: This game should never be played with a child under ten. For kids over ten, they can drop a handful of treats on the ground then run away. When their puppy starts to run toward them, they drop more treats then turn and run in another direction. The dropping of the treats helps create a natural break in the excitement level, reducing the possibility of over excitement and possible accidents.

Nusa and I playing recall games

Otis and I working on his leash skills

Auto practices his attention skills.

Lady and Jojen share a toy during play.

Caring for The Whole Puppy   97

This book is just the beginning!

Raising a puppy is serious business and should be treated as such. The effort and commitment you put in now will reap big benefits in the long run. One of the biggest reasons adolescent dogs are surrendered to shelters in such great numbers is due to lack of or improper early socialization and training. Making the time to properly train and socialize your puppy now, means life with him later will be much easier and more enjoyable.

I hope I have given you some fun and exciting ideas on how to make raising your new puppy easier and more fulfilling for you, your puppy and your whole family. I can't stress enough how important these early weeks are in your developing puppy's life and how important these foundations are to creating your ideal companion dog. We can teach sit at any age. Teaching your puppy that the world is not a scary place needs to happen first!

There is so much information on raising puppies and dog training in general. Not all of it is accurate and a lot of it is contradictory. It is very difficult to figure out what information is going to help you the best. I have created this resource list to help you get further information on positive reinforcement training, puppy development, and socialization.

> Feel free to contact me as well with any questions you may have at wickedgooddogtraining@gmail.com or check out my FB page Erica Marshall Cpdt-ka

Resources

About the Author

Misti Fry Cpdt-ka

Sidekick Dog Training www.springfieldsidekickdogtraining.com

and

MVP K9 Coach www.mvpk9coach.com

Humane Society of Southwest Missouri www.swh.org

Rutland County Humane Society www.rchsvt.org

Chapter 2

Orthopedic Foundation for Animals www.ofa.org

American Kennel Club www.akc.org

Dominance and Dog Training www.apdt.org/resource-center/dominance-and-dog-training

Dominance Position Statement by the American Veterinary Society of Animal Behaviorists

www.avsab.org under resources and position statements

Dog Food Advisor www.dogfoodadvisor.com

Puppia harness www.puppiaus.com

Bark Appeal harness www.barkappeal.com

Freedom Harness www.2houndsdesign.com

Chapter 3

American Veterinary Medical Association www.avma.org

American Animal Hospital Association www.aaha.org

Fear Free Pets www.fearfreepets.com

Association of Professional Dog Trainers www.apdt.com

The Certification Council of Professional Dog Trainers www.ccpdt.com

International Association of Animal Behavior Consultants www.iaabc.com

Professional Animal Care Certification Council www.paccert.com

Chapter 4

Learning Theory www.allpetseducationandtraining.com.au/learning-theory.html

'Learning theory' terminology: classical and operant conditioning
https://behaviourvet.wordpress.com/2013/10/12/learning-theory-terminology-classical-and-operant-conditioning/

The ABC's of Dog Training https://www.doggieresidence.com/2017/11/28/abcs-dog-training/

The Importance of Socialization https://apdt.com/resource-center/the-importance-of-socialization/

Sound Proof Puppy Training app https://apps.apple.com/us/app/sound-proof-puppy-training/id700513321

Susan Garret Crate Games on YouTube https://youtu.be/L8HNO79bZMY

Mine by Jean Donaldson

https://www.dogwise.com/mine-a-practical-guide-to-resource-guarding-in-dogs/

Wicked Good Dog Training YouTube channel https://www.youtube.com/channel/UCowH9yF6yHCRI-kugeDQNqA

Chapter 6

Kong https://www.kongcompany.com/

Pet Safe toys https://www.petsafe.net/toys

Nina Ottosson toys https://www.nina-ottosson.com

Outward hound toys https://outwardhound.com

TuffieToys https://tuffietoys.com

Tether Tug www.tethertug.com

Jolly Pets toys www.jollypets.com

JW Pet toys https://www.petmate.com/brands/jw/category/brand-jw

Animal Muscle Release Therapy

Exercises for Young Dogs https://www.animal-mrt.com/blog/post/21701/Exercises-for-Young-Dogs/

Avidog-Zink Ventures

Fit For Life Puppy Exercise Book https://www.avidogzink.com/shop/dog-exercise-books-posters-videos/fit-for-life-puppy-exercise-book/

Chapter 7

Canine Body Language A Photographic Guide by Brenda Aloff

https://www.dogwise.com/canine-body-language-a-photographic-guide/

On Talking Terms With Dogs —Calming Signals by Turid Rugaas

https://www.dogwise.com/on-talking-terms-with-dogs-calming-signals-2nd-edition/

The Family Dog —Stop the 77

https://www.thefamilydog.com/stop-the-77/

For further information check out these leaders in the field of behavior and training

Dr Patricia MCconnell https://www.patriciamcconnell.com

Jean Donaldson www.academyfordogtrainers.com

Dr. Christopher Pachel https://www.instinctdogtraining.com/personnel/chris-pachel/

Karen Pryor www.clickertraining.com

Dr. Susan Friedman www.behaviorworks.org

Nicole Wilde www.nicolewilde.com

Websites to visit

Family Paws www.familypaws.com

The Pet Professional Guild www.petprofessionalguild.com

Whole Dog Journal www.wholedogjournal.com

American College of Veterinary Behaviorists https://www.dacvb.org

Other Media Resources

Reisner Veterinary Behavior http://reisnervetbehavior.com/blog/

Barking Brains https://www.facebook.com/neuroscienceisawesome/

Hannah Brannigan

Drinking From The Toilet https://hannahbranigan.dog/dog-training-podcast/

Behavior Vets https://www.facebook.com/VBCCO/

Author Thanks

I would first like to thank all the trainers before me that mentored and guided me either personally or through their work in the field of behavior and training. Lesli Hyland, Misti Fry and Carrie Galvan got me on the path and luminaries like Sue Sternberg and Patricia McConnell led me along with their amazing knowledge and body of work.

I am so grateful for the amazing friends I have made along this journey of working with dogs in so many capacities. Trainers that taught me and my dogs along the way like Amee Abel, Rachel Brostrom and Diane Gibbons were invaluable to furthering my knowledge and excitement for working with dogs and their people. Countless friends have been made within competition venues and rescue work, so many it's hard to list. Suffice it to say that if you met me through working with our dogs, you have had an impact on my life.

Chris Johnson took me in and gave me a place to develop my teaching skills and curriculum writing. Working with her allowed me to acquire my needed hours for my certification and to try out new classes and formats. I am forever grateful for her guidance and support as I built my confidence and my business.

All the wonderful client friends I have made through my business have really helped bring about this book. Their faith in me and their willingness to work with their dogs in a positive manner helped me strengthen my belief in the curriculum and programs I was building, not to mention being entrusted with their beloved pups, it was such an honor to help you all.

The many adorable photos in this book were graciously provided to me by Janet Hopkins, Marie Silverberg, Lesli Hyland, Cassidy Albert and Ariane Bailey. Many thanks, ladies!

I would like to thank the wonderfully supportive community of Peterborough NH. I appreciate all the businesses that welcomed me and the puppies I was working with. Places like Agway, Steele's Stationers, Belletete's, Ava Marie's Handmade Chocolates and The Toadstool Bookshop. Also thanks to Lisa Betz and Lauren Martin at the local recreation department for being so welcoming to me and my group classes. I am indebted to you all.

To the wonderful friends and family that read the first drafts of this book, Seren Maxwell, Bridget Feldbaum and Lesli Hyland, thank you for your words of encouragement and support and your willingness to correct my grammar!

To my husband and children who bore the brunt of my being gone teaching classes, volunteering at the shelter or meeting private lesson clients, thank you for your understanding and support. I couldn't have succeeded without your support.

To my children, Rylie and Caitlin, for being a part of my training process with puppies and other dogs in classes or in our home. You both made my job so much easier and I am so proud of the smart and compassionate young adults you are growing into.

And to the dog who started it all, Beanie. Gone, but never forgotten and loved eternally.

www.ingramcontent.com/pod-product-compliance
Lightning Source LLC
Chambersburg PA
CBHW041215070526
44579CB00001B/4